UNDER ONE UMBRELLA

May God Bless you & use you

Love, Carol

UNDER ONE UMBRELLA

PATRICIA HAMP | CAROL ROSENBERG

A Division of WINEPRESS PUBLISHING

© 2007 by Patricia Hamp & Carol Rosenberg. All rights reserved.

Pleasant Word (a division of WinePress Publishing, PO Box 428, Enumclaw, WA 98022) functions only as book publisher. As such, the ultimate design, content, editorial accuracy, and views expressed or implied in this work are those of the author.

No part of this publication may be reproduced, stored in a retrieval system, or transmitted in any way by any means—electronic, mechanical, photocopy, recording, or otherwise—without the prior permission of the copyright holder, except as provided by USA copyright law.

Unless otherwise noted, all Scriptures are taken from the Holy Bible, New International Version, Copyright © 1973, 1978, 1984 by the International Bible Society. Used by permission of Zondervan Publishing House. The "NIV" and "New International Version" trademarks are registered in the United States Patent and Trademark Office by International Bible Society.

Scripture references marked KJV are taken from the King James Version of the Bible.

Scripture references marked NASB are taken from the New American Standard Bible, © 1960, 1963, 1968, 1971, 1972, 1973, 1975, 1977 by The Lockman Foundation. Used by permission.

ISBN 13: 978-1-4141-0872-8
ISBN 10: 1-4141-0872-9
Library of Congress Catalog Card Number: 2006908896

THIS BOOK IS DEDICATED TO

OUR FAMILY

SPECIAL THANKS

TO OUR HUSBANDS

FOR GOD GIVING CAROL AND PAT A TRUE
FRIENDSHIP THAT PASSES ALL UNDERSTANDING.

TABLE OF CONTENTS

Introduction: Just Singing in the Rain ix

1. Don't Open Your Umbrella Indoors 13
2. Raindrops Keep Falling on My Head 19
3. Stormy Weather 23
4. My Pot of Gold 33
5. Sun Out, Umbrella Down 37
6. Just Two More Raindrops 41
7. Every Cloud Has a Silver Lining
   (Or Is That Aluminum?) 45
8. Our Umbrella Is Up 49
9. Who Needs an Umbrella? 55
10. I Knew, That I Knew, That I Knew 63
11. The Ribs That Hold the Umbrella Up 69
12. Move That Umbrella Over, Please 75

Afterword: Somewhere over the Rainbow 91

INTRODUCTION: JUST SINGING IN THE RAIN

Um.brel.la: protection device from the elements of your life.

Oh, what a klutz you are!

I tried in vain to steady the teetering Waterford crystal goblets as they tipped out of the box I was carrying. The sound of glass shattering on polished hardwood floors echoed in the nearly empty dining room. I looked around at Pat's beautiful crystal scattered all over the floor and felt sick to my stomach. I had come to help my friend pack as she and her husband Gary were moving again. As I carried in three boxes piled on top of each other, I caught my toe on the edge of the rug and stumbled. The delicate glass goblets had flown outward in a glittering radius.

Pat, who had been upstairs packing up the books that Gary wanted to keep, heard the crash and started down the stairs.

"Carol, what's all that racket down there?" I was relieved to hear her voice sounding more curious than upset. "Sounds like you're having a toast and throwing the glasses into the fireplace for effect."

As my friend Pat came down the steps into the dining room I began apologizing. "I'm really sorry; I'm really sorry," I kept saying. It was as if I were seeking a pardon for a crime before the victim even had a clue as to what happened.

We were good enough friends that I knew Pat would know I was truly worried by the way I kept saying how sorry I was.

"What have you gone and done now?" Pat asked me in mock disapproval. She likes to play the tough guy sometimes.

I looked up at her from the floor where I was picking up pieces of crystal. I couldn't tell from the look on her face how she really felt. Beads of sweat were forming on my forehead. "I broke your Waterford," I confessed.

Pat looked around the dining room at the shattered pieces of two of her favorite Waterford goblets. "Is this why you look so worried? It's just two pieces—we've got lots more! You know Gary, every time we move we have to buy new stuff." She laughed and said, "After thirteen moves, we're loaded with crystal and china."

Just as I was beginning to feel relieved, I thought about Pat's husband, Gary, who enjoys all the beautiful things that Pat and he collect. "What will Gary say? You know he doesn't like anyone touching his stuff, and here you entrust me with your Waterford!"

"Please, don't worry," Pat said. "He's hundreds of miles away in Florida. All this stuff is going on the moving truck, so who knows what they might break? Anyway, I don't think he counts the pieces we have. He probably won't notice."

I wasn't quite ready to stop worrying. "I just feel terrible. I'll replace those two pieces."

"Don't be ridiculous," Pat insisted. "They're only things!" She laughed and said, "Friends are more important than things any day," and started back up the stairs.

I watched Pat, my friend, and thought about the journey we had shared together. We were friends against all odds. She is way more than just a friend. She is part of our extended family. Our history is entwined. In fact, she was my husband's first wife.

But, that's another story.

Chapter 1

DON'T OPEN YOUR UMBRELLA INDOORS

PAT

As I walked up the stairs I thought about our friendship. I knew it was unusual. My best friend is married to my first husband. She's here helping me pack up so I can join my second husband in Florida. She is the third wife of my first husband and he is her second husband. Could it be any more confusing than that? It's amazing how God has made something so painful into something beautiful.

I'd better get back to work. I had just started wedging books into yet another box when one of the books in a stack I was packing fell open. Onto the carpet dropped some forgotten pictures of my sons, Mark, Matthew and Mitch when they were very little. I sat down and stared at the pictures of my cute boys, dressed in their little suits. Turning over another photo I saw those three small boys, this time with their father. He looks so young and handsome. Just like the day I met him.

That day, many years before, I was sitting on the porch watching traffic go by. I certainly didn't know that I was about to meet the new man—or should I say boy?—in my life. I mean,

I was only fifteen! When you're fifteen what do you know about love?

I was sitting there, minding my own business, when I happened to look across the street to the house where I occasionally babysat the children. The door opened and a young man came outside. Who was that and why was he there? That was my babysitting job! I gave it a few minutes and then wandered over nonchalantly to see what I could find out.

"Hi, I'm Pat."

"I'm David."

I discovered David Rosenberg was the uncle of the kids I took care of. We talked for a while and I thought this uncle guy didn't seem too bad. He went to a different high school than I did, and that was intriguing to me. Right then I began to like him.

"Would you like to go get something to eat with me tomorrow?" David asked.

"Sure." I knew I'd have to get permission from my parents first, but said yes anyway. At fifteen I had not really gone anywhere with a boy. That night my parents said yes, with the stipulation that someone else had to come along with us.

The next day David picked me up in his dad's car with a friend in the back seat. David later told me that his friend's job was to hold the car door so it wouldn't rattle!

That was the beginning of my new life with David Rosenberg. I thought I was in love. I didn't really know what love was, but I thought this was it for sure! We went together from the ninth grade on, and all through high school. We'd go to the dances and proms and a few school activities in each other's schools. He really didn't like coming to my school but he came anyway. He really didn't like going to his school either.

My dad said David was a "hood." I didn't understand why my dad thought that, although I secretly thought he looked a lot like Elvis.

David and Pat at 16 & 15

One year after we had graduated from high school we decided to get married. Actually, it was the fact that I was pregnant that decided it for us. It was the month of April. The timing wasn't good, as my older sister was planning her wedding for June. David and I decided to elope, and asked our friends to go with us up north. We got our papers ready and took our blood tests, shaking in our boots all the way. We told our parents we were going to the movies. Instead we headed up north to David's parents' cottage where we had gone on occasion.

Arriving in Kalkaska, Michigan, about 9:30 P.M., we found the justice of the peace in the hotel bar. After we produced our paperwork he agreed to marry us. He was also an insurance agent, so we went to his office where he married us. By 10:30 P.M. we were legal and hungry and went off to get something to eat. Our wedding night was spent in a twelve-dollar-a-night motel room, not quite first class.

When we called home, David's parents were fine with it. Mine were in disbelief that I could do such a thing. We were not looking forward to coming home, but when we did my parents seemed to be over the shock.

Our life together had begun. For forty dollars a month we rented a furnished apartment. David was working at a gas station part time and going to school part time. I was working at a local bank. Even with both jobs, we had all we could do to keep our heads above water.

Our son was born. Then the next year I found I was pregnant with my second baby. David? Well, he was busy trying to have a life. He never seemed to realize what marriage is all about. You go to work, take care of the kids, fix dinner, get the laundry done and then go to bed. What was so hard about that? He had decided to find much more exciting things to do.

By the third year we had three boys and our marriage was not doing too well. For me the routine really was all about work—taking care of the kids, doing the laundry, and then dropping into bed. If David wanted to do something else he did it by himself. There was not a whole lot of money for a babysitter. Anyway, I didn't really relish going out drinking beer and sitting around talking about nothing.

Where there is love, there is always hope. Our love life was fine. A friend told me, "If you're having sex, things must be OK." The problem was he was having sex with many other women and I didn't know it. Or maybe I just didn't want to know it!

We moved to Indian River and went into business for ourselves with a home improvement company.

After a few years of all work and kids, we separated. So many things had happened in our marriage that we felt we couldn't reconcile. I packed up the three boys and off I went to start over on my own. After all, I thought, I need to be happy. I got an apartment in Lansing, put the boys in school, and stayed home to take care of them. I didn't have to work because David paid all the bills and he wanted me home with the boys. After a year of him coming down on the weekends, unless work kept him up north, we decided to get back together. He was going to be better and I was going to be more understanding. We both agreed the boys needed two parents.

We bought a nice home on the north side of Lansing. Our business was up and running again and our family back on track. The new friends we met all had families, and soon we were spending time together. On the weekends we would all get together and party. Everyone came over to our house, as we had a swimming pool. Life was good. The boys were doing well and everybody was happy…at least I thought we were.

David began selling real estate part time at a local firm while still keeping the home improvement business going. We'd socialize with the people he worked with and also our neighbors. David would often be out until the wee hours of the morning. If I asked where he was, he would always tell me he was working, selling a roof, siding, windows or something. Things were getting real bad. He'd come home drunk. He seemed angry at himself and he'd start fights. To escape, at times I would go across the street, if I could get away. I didn't want the boys to hear us, not to mention the entire neighborhood.

Late one night he came home drunk. I had all the doors locked so he started banging on the front door. I finally jumped up and went to the door in my nightgown. When I wouldn't let him in, he pulled the screen door open and grabbed me and dragged me out into the yard. In the process of our tussle he pulled my nightgown over my head and I started to scream. The next-door neighbors woke up to see me stark naked on my front lawn. Finally, I got him into the house. Exhausted, we sat down and both started to laugh.

Later when I thought about that incident, a quote from Agatha Christie came to mind: "I like living. I have sometimes been wildly, despairingly, acutely miserable, racked with sorrow, but through it all, I still know quite certainly that just to be alive is a grand thing."

This went on for months. Our friends tried to help us but we didn't listen to them. After all, they were not doing too well themselves.

Then something happened that gave our marriage a death blow.

Chapter 2

RAINDROPS KEEP FALLING ON MY HEAD

PAT

I found out that David had been seeing Betty, a girl at his real estate office, for some time. When he came home one night I asked him about her.

"We're just friends. Sometimes I have to stay over there at night because she is going through a divorce. I'm her only friend."

I thought I'd better take a look in the mirror because I didn't think I looked that stupid!

"You have to leave!" I yelled. "I am not going to live like this again." The kids and I deserved better. I knew the boys had just about had enough. It was better for their dad to leave than us living with the uncertainty and tension of not knowing when he was coming home and in what condition.

David left. Several weeks passed and he stopped by and said he wanted to come home. He and Betty were finished. We talked into the night and decided to try again—for the boys.

Early the next morning a friend came by in his black sports car. Ned said he wanted to take me on a ride and show me something. Ned and his wife, Sandy, were among our closest friends. We partied together and would go out together often for a meal. I knew that Ned and Sandy weren't getting along too well and wondered why he didn't take care of his own family. But that morning I thought I'd go on that ride. He seemed to sincerely want to help me.

He drove me to a house in a quiet neighborhood and asked me to go up to the door. I thought this is a strange thing he is asking me to do, but I was curious. I walked up to the door and rang the doorbell, all the while looking around me at the perfectly ordinary surroundings.

The door opened. A tall, slender woman stood there. It was Betty! She took one look at me and started screaming into the house at David. Nobody had said I couldn't come in, so in I went. She was still screaming in the kitchen when David came up to me and asked, "What are you doing here?"

In a loud voice so everyone could hear, I said, "Last night you promised you'd give this up and come home for the boys and the family." I said whatever I could think of to say at the time, seeing as how I had the floor.

It was clear that Betty didn't know anything about the night before. She began to race around the kitchen out of control, waving her long arms and pointing her long, manicured red fingernails at David, screaming, "Get her out of here."

"Pat, go!"

"Are you sure you really want it this way?"

"Get out of here, you…"

David called me a name that was more technically correct applied to a female dog, but it was plain that he was talking to me. I got the message and walked out without another word. When I got back into Ned's car I told him what happened in Betty's kitchen, and also what had happened the night before. I could tell he felt bad, but he thought I should see for myself what David was up to. I guess he was right—I had to see for myself to believe it. I cried all the way home and wondered, "Am I crying over this relationship for the last time?"

Chapter 3

STORMY WEATHER

PAT

Back home I somehow got through the normal morning routines. I got the boys off to school and picked up around the house. Finally, I had to face myself. I sat down in the living room and asked myself, "Am I happy?" Desperate to talk to someone I called my Aunt Betty, who was often my port in a storm. Betty was a positive person with a lot of wisdom. After I finished my story, she gave me a name and number of her attorney.

I made that phone call and got an appointment for the first of the week. *I just want to get on with my life,* I thought.

That night the boys and I sat down and talked. Mark was eleven, Matthew ten, and Mitchell eight years old. They had all been through a lot over the past five years. The boys were sad, and listened with tears glistening in their eyes. But, even at their young ages they weren't devastated, and seemed to know divorce would be better for all of us. We just couldn't keep going on as we were.

"I still love your dad, but I'm just not 'in love' with him anymore," I told them. "He's welcome to come over to our house anytime to see you. You guys will be able to go with him whenever you want." I told them the only thing I did not want was to see Betty coming up my driveway. We would not talk about her. I felt it was up to them how they wanted to think about her. I could have given them a few opinions, but I didn't.

After that night, not much was said about us splitting up. It made me sad to see the hurt on their young faces. I knew that no matter how bad our troubled situation was, in their young hearts there was still a part of them that thought it would get better. I knew communication was crucial. We made a promise to each other to take time to talk to make sure everyone was OK.

The house took on a different feeling after that night. Over and over I played the song "I am Woman" by Helen Reddy. I'm sure my boys wondered what train I was on. At dinnertime it was a relief not to be waiting for David and worrying about if he would show up. The boys pitched in, kept the lawn mowed, helped with dinner, cleaned the pool, and did a lot of things I never asked them to do. We all grew up a little. It was as if the boys seemed to know this was the last time we were going through this.

David's role changed with the boys. He called often to check on the boys and to see if his sons had everything they needed. If there was something they needed, he made sure they got it. All of a sudden he took on being dad with a capital D. Maybe he was always Dad—he just didn't seem to know where his home was most of the time.

When I told David that I had seen an attorney and he would be getting divorce papers soon, he seemed to take it well…that is, until he got the papers. The night he was served he came over drunk.

"I didn't think it was going to happen so fast," he said. He seemed not to think that it was even going to happen at all. Part of me felt so sorry for him. He was torn between his family and what he thought he really wanted.

He talked to the boys for a while before he left. It seemed to go OK. But, I wondered, how can this confusing mess ever be OK? How can any child understand and handle hearing his dad say he doesn't love his mom anymore and doesn't want to live at home where you are? Thank God children survive their parents!

David moved in with Betty. Just about every weekend the boys went over there. When they came home, I tried not to ask how things were going. I was curious and wasn't upset when the boys let slip that things were not going too well. Betty did not like the idea that whatever the boys wanted, they got. Maybe she thought she was taking second place. Mitch (our youngest) said she would be hot one moment and cold the next. He never knew what to expect. She would fly into a rage and start screaming. Betty also had a younger son who she felt didn't get treated like David's boys did. She wanted things to change and right now. I soon learned that right now were some of Betty's favorite words.

My actions didn't help their relationship. David told me, "If there is anything you or the boys need, don't hesitate to call me." Well, it's so easy to be wicked without being consciously aware of our motivations, isn't it? Things just kept popping up that I needed. I'd call David at any time of the day or night when I needed something. Sure enough, he would come over and help me.

Of course, this did not set too well with Betty. Her needs didn't set too well with me either. I was convinced that the what-goes-around-comes-around philosophy was right. The boys would report that their dad and Betty were fighting more and more. One day David came over to swim with the boys. When he took his shirt off, I noticed he had scratch marks up and down his back. I felt bad, but not bad enough not to ask him, "How many cats did you have to fight off?" He just smiled.

I think it was then and there that David and I, without even knowing it, made the decision that, no matter what, we would remain friends.

As weeks went by, David would stop in to say hi or to check on how things were going. He was always welcome, as long as he behaved himself. One night he stopped in as we were about to sit down for dinner and asked if he could stay. Of course, the boys and I said yes. He started to go over to where he had always sat at the head of the table. Mark, our oldest boy, spoke up and said, "Dad, you don't sit there anymore. I'm the head of the house now." David didn't say anything; he just sat down in another chair.

I realized that night that Mark was taking on too much. He was trying to be the dad. It was time to have a talk and to let him know that he was not responsible or in charge of the family. He seemed to understand, and he eased up after that. He told me that night that he always felt bad that he couldn't help me more when his dad was being bad to me. As we cried together, he said that he knew he wasn't big enough to help.

I felt terrible to think that my young son was carrying such a memory. What do we put our children through and not even know it, because we are so busy trying to keep ourselves together?

A few years later Mark joined a gym and soon became Mr. Teen Michigan in a bodybuilding competition. I wondered if the motivation for him getting involved in bodybuilding was related to this trauma in his life.

I wanted the divorce settlement to be done in a business-like way. But I knew I would only get one chance, so it needed to be the best settlement I could get. We started to go through the inventory of our property. I wanted to keep the house and everything in it except his personal things. After all, David was the one who had a vested interest in getting this divorce through in a hurry. He agreed. He wanted the business and everything in it. I fully understood that he had to work so he could pay support.

Support became the big issue when we went to court the first time to determine the terms. He insisted that he was not going to pay to the "friend of the court." Nobody was going to tell him how he had to take care of his children! He was a responsible father. The judge wasn't happy with this, but he said he would go along with it as long as I agreed. I didn't have a problem with it as long as he was not late with his payments. The agreement was if he was late, I could go back to the judge for another ruling. Back and forth the settlement proceedings went on with small details. Months went by.

Betty was getting nervous. The divorce proceedings were not happening as fast as she thought they should.

One day I got a call from my Aunt Betty who was close friends with my attorney. She informed me that my attorney had just died of a heart attack. While dancing with his wife he had just dropped over. We were back to square one. I had to find a new attorney, and all the papers had to be transferred over to him. This took another month.

As the divorce moved along, I knew that the rest of my life needed to move along as well. I knew I needed to make a living. After deliberating, I decided to sell real estate. The hours were flexible and I could be home when the boys were. I thought this career would also give me a lot of free time to find myself. I was no longer David's wife. I had a new life and I definitely needed to find myself. With this decision I felt as if my life was back on track.

I passed my real estate exam and found a company at which to place my license.

The divorce was still pending. But David and I couldn't seem to cut it off cleanly. The boys and I allowed him to come around even when he had had a little too much to drink. At times he would be in a violent mood. Sometimes I would run across the street to my friend's house and she would call the police. Strangely enough, the same police officer would always come. Finally, he told me that I might want to talk to my attorney about a restraining order. I did get one, but it didn't work because David always took off before the police got there.

David was so good to us when he wasn't drinking that it made it hard to keep my resolve with him when he was. I felt he was conflicted and confused about what he was doing. He was like someone who had his foot stuck into a mud hole and couldn't pull himself out.

Maybe that's why we always stayed friends. Of course, it was because of the boys too. I never felt they deserved the divorce. The problem was just between their dad and me.

It wasn't too long before the policeman who often answered my calls began stopping by during the day to see how things were going. He was a lot of fun, and soon we started a relationship. I was ready for a little fun. The best part was that he seemed to really care about the boys and me. He helped me a lot with them and they really liked him.

There was one minor problem…he was married! But he said he wasn't happy at home and was planning on getting a divorce. I wish I could say that when I heard he was married that was the end of our relationship. But it wasn't. Of course, that made matters worse. David said it wasn't right for me to be seeing a married man. He said he made that mistake and I shouldn't be breaking up a home.

Months went by before we got the call to go to court. David called me and we went together like old friends. After we signed the papers we had lunch together and then he dropped me off at my home. My home. "Your house is your home only when you feel you have jurisdiction over the space," says Joan Krona. For me, the moment was bittersweet.

A few months after our divorce was finalized, David and Betty married. The boys were not too happy, but they needed to give it a chance. They went with their dad every weekend up north to the cottage, kicking and screaming at times, but they went. Their dad insisted they go, so they did. They'd come home and tell me how bad it was there as David and Betty fought all the time.

Meanwhile, I was still seeing my policeman friend. I felt I was having a great time. I was his one and only. Then I found out that I wasn't his only one and only! I began seeing other men, but I always came back to him.

I still called David when I needed things done, and he came anytime I called. The boys remained really important to him, and he stopped in when he wanted to see them.

It seemed to me that things were not going too well for him and Betty. Sometimes if you set out to shoot yourself in the foot, you might miss and hit your heart. Well, this is what happened to Betty. She seemed to be losing ground fast. You should never go against the thing that means the most to a person that you love, that is, if you want to win. Life was not easy for Betty. She was having a hard time accepting what was coming between her and David. Of course, as soon as the gun was empty, I would hand her a new box of shells. Why? I don't really know why. I guess it was because I had suffered a living death and I didn't think she deserved my husband or my boys. I didn't want my husband anymore, but my boys didn't deserve her for a stepmother. I didn't know if I was in the wrong for the death of their marriage, or if it was going to happen anyway. I do feel that it was partly my doing.

About one year into their marriage Betty said she couldn't handle the boys anymore. She told David he had to make a choice. Well, his choice was divorce. That made two divorces for David. Was I happy? Not really, but the boys were. David did seem relieved. I knew there was someone out there for David and my boys, and that he was bound to find her.

Little did I know then that Carol would be the someone who would become his wife, and that we would become best friends.

Two years went by and David continued stopping in anytime he wanted to see the boys. Our friendship was still very strong. But there was never any talk about us getting back together. It seemed that we both knew that wasn't what either of us wanted.

He never said anything, but I had the feeling he was seeing Betty off and on, probably trying to get her through the divorce. David always was one to help out the lonely and desperate. I didn't think she needed the help. After all, she got the large home and half of his half he had left over from me and the kids. I would tell him you can only slice the pie so many times until you end up with an empty pie plate. But David worked hard and always ended up back on top. God certainly had His hand on David's life.

I was still dating my married policeman friend off and on. It was strange on the occasions when all of us—me and the boys—were getting ready to go out on dates. Finally, the man I was dating got a divorce and got married—but not to me! I felt terrible at first, but now I thank the Lord it wasn't me.

One evening David called. "Can I bring a friend over to meet you?" he asked. The friend turned out to be the new woman in his life. Of course I wanted to meet her! I had no idea on that first meeting how much the new woman in David's life would change my life. I liked her from the minute she came in the door. She was so different from anyone David had dated. She and I had a great talk. It didn't take me long to know—probably before David did—that she was the one for him. It made me feel good that David included me, but I wasn't too surprised that he did. That's how our friendship was.

I was thrilled when I saw David and Carol hitting it off. After they dated for a while, they asked me to go on outings or to school activities with them. For me, I had just gained a friend. Carol's son, John, was a great kid. He was a little younger than my boys, but they all seemed to like each other.

The time came for me to sell the house and get something that wasn't so much work. When I listed the house, the boys and I felt sad. But the house was just too much work. Since the boys were not around so much, I couldn't do it anymore.

In two months the house sold. I moved into a condo in DeWitt and enjoyed not worrying about the yard and maintenance. The boys seemed fine with this change, as they were busy with their own lives. We still tried to have our dinners together and our talks.

When the boys began graduating from high school I knew I wanted to settle down. I had just about enough of this dating stuff. Settling down and getting married again began to sound attractive to me. But I didn't want someone who had young children. I had already raised my own and they didn't need a father—they already had one, and a good one. I needed someone to love me and to be a good friend to my boys. I was prepared to be a friend to his, if he had older children.

I didn't know then that there was a big change coming in my life, and coming fast.

Chapter 4

MY POT OF GOLD

PAT

The door of our office opened and in walked a man in a leather sports coat and western boots. He was tall, had dark hair, broad shoulders, big brown eyes, nice teeth and great hands. My heart was beating so fast I had to sit down. One look and I was in love! I took a deep breath and told myself, "Get a grip, girl." His name was Gary and he asked to see the manager. I was the assistant manager so I walked him back to the manager's office next to mine.

I found out Gary was moving into the city from Charlevoix and needed to place his broker's license with a company. He happened to know someone who worked in my office, so he had come there. What a break, I thought.

The bad part was that he was dating the person he knew in the office. He was also in the process of a divorce. Well, this had never stopped me before, and it sure was not getting in my way now. As the weeks went by we became friends. The woman he was dating, and the guy I was dating, decided we would all go out on a double date. That night we got to know each other a little better, but not well enough for me! Gary was so nice and so sweet, not like me. I'm a little more outspoken and open.

When my August birthday rolled around Gary called me to wish me "happy birthday." He had asked his girlfriend to send me a card and sign both of their names to it. I got the card, alright, but hers was the only name on it. A day or so later I had the office over for breakfast before we went out to look at open houses. The birthday card was propped up on the fireplace mantle. Gary went over to look at it and noticed his name wasn't on the card. He seemed upset. His girlfriend had told him she put both of their names on it. Not a good move on her part.

A month later it was time for our office party, a family affair. Gary's friend, who had two children, didn't want her children to know she was dating. So she asked me if I would bring him. She'd meet him at the party. Naturally, I agreed to do her that favor. It was about a two-hour drive to the park so I had some time to really get to know him. I really wanted Gary to get to know me. The day went fine. I was just myself. The ride was pleasant, the sun was shining, the air was fresh and clear, and I had a couple of hours to talk with Gary.

He spent the day with his girlfriend in the park. Me? I looked at my watch every hour until it was time to take him home.

"Are you hungry?" Gary asked on the way home. Of course I was. We stopped and got a pizza and had a few glasses of wine. It was the perfect setting for two people to get to know each other a better—a little pizza and a lot of wine and a girl who had stars in her eyes. And we did get better acquainted. The next day Gary stopped by and we talked. By the following week, Gary had left his girlfriend and we started a relationship.

I was ecstatic. Gary was just what I wanted in a husband. Soon we started talking about marriage. I knew that I had to tell Gary about my friendship with my ex-husband David and his new wife, Carol. I didn't know what he was going to think about all of it. But, he was the love of my life and my soon-to-be husband. When I talked to him, I told him how David and I had remained friends after the divorce. Then I told him how David met Carol and how the three of us became friends. He seemed OK with it.

We made plans to have dinner with David and Carol so Gary could get to know them. The dinner went great. Gary seemed to like the two of them and we hit it off as a foursome. It wasn't long until we were doing more together and David and Carol had become Gary's friends too.

A few months later, Gary and I were married in a wonderful wedding. "Thank you, God, for staying with me and sending me the man of my dreams," I breathed as I walked down the aisle. All our children were in the ceremony. My oldest son Mark walked me down the aisle. Gary's oldest son Greg was the best man, and my other two boys were the groomsmen. His daughter Vickie was my bridesmaid, along with my sisters, and one of my friends was my maid of honor. His two children, his daughter Vickie and son Greg, and my three boys, Mark, Matthew, and Mitch were all close in age and all on their own. We were a happy, blended family.

Chapter 5

SUN OUT, UMBRELLA DOWN

Gary

When I met Pat my life was in turmoil. My wife had left me and filed for divorce. I had hoped to go to seminary, but those plans were shattered. My daughter Vickie had just gotten married, and my son Greg had moved into an apartment with a friend. Our home was up for sale, and my real estate business sold. Life just kept getting worse. I decided to move to Lansing and start classes at Michigan State University. So I put my broker's license with a real estate firm there and began the task of getting my life back on track.

That's when I met Pat. My first impression of her was not all that favorable. I thought she was a "brassy broad." I was dating Marsha, a friend in my office to whom my sister had introduced me. In fact, Marsha thought Pat was her best friend.

In time Pat and I fell in love. I shared with her my sense of a "call" to the ministry, thoughts of seminary, and my love of God and what I wanted to do with my life. I told her that I wanted her to be part of it. When Pat was open to this huge lifestyle change, I felt great joy. I was so happy to find someone that I felt comfortable with and had so much in common with.

Pat shared with me that she was not just *friends* with David and his wife Carol, but *best* friends. She wanted me to meet them and be a part of that relationship. In a way it seemed strange, but I was intrigued and I knew how important it was to her. So I thought—why not? It was strange at first, but in time we began doing things together and it was fine.

After we married, my life felt like it was back on track.

David and I talked and shared our faith together. We probably couldn't have been further apart theologically, but we learned what we could talk about and what to stay away from. When Pat and I decided to go to the General Theological Seminary in Manhattan he was happy for us. He did think that Pat should stay with him and Carol while I was in New York. He was convinced the world would be coming to a terrible end and he didn't want Pat stranded in a large metropolitan city when disaster struck. But we worked through that and Pat and I went off to New York City to seminary.

David and Carol came to visit us on more than one occasion. At my ordination to the priesthood I asked David to be a presenter. David has always played a part in my ministry, and I in his. He asked me to have a role in his ordination into the ministry at Bear Lake Church in Michigan.

Our lives have taken us to so many places. Who would have thought that my wife's ex-husband would play such an important part in my life and I in his life? As the years have gone by (over twenty-seven) we have done a lot together. David and Carol have visited us everywhere we have been. He has asked me to speak at his church at different times. Our youth group has gone up to his place in northern Michigan for a weekend. We have shared our ups and downs in life and ministry.

Our relationship has been an experience in forgiveness that has become so much more. Our friendship has helped me in my life. All our children have gained a great deal from the four of us being friends. Our families and friends at times have thought we were all a bit weird. But how can it be weird when there's love and a friendship beyond belief? Yes, Carol and Pat have a wonderful friendship. But David and I have a great one too, not to mention the relationship that the four of us have.

David on the left and Gary on the Right

Chapter 6

JUST TWO MORE RAINDROPS

Pat

"Hey, you girls, how are you doing?" My neighbor and friend Sandy waved at us from her deck. "Come on over," she called.

As we walked over to their house, I told Carol, "Ken and Sandy have been the best neighbors. When we moved from church to church they have taken care of the house. On the day we moved in, Sandy brought us over cookies and something cold to drink."

As Sandy welcomed Carol and me with a cool drink, I thought how Ken had helped Gary with projects around the house, and how he kept an eye on the place. We had been gone for two years when we got a new assignment in Florida. We were hoping to come back, so we kept the house. The house sat with all our things in it for two years. Ken and Sandy watched over it as if it were their own for all that time. They weeded and made sure the yard was taken care of. They'd even check the inside of the house. If a light bulb needed to be replaced, they'd do it. We talked to them every few weeks to see how things were going.

Out on Sandy's deck I reintroduced Carol to her.

"Oh yes, I remember meeting you over a Thanksgiving weekend. You and your husband were here with the rest of the family. You're Pat's first husband's wife, right?"

Carol hesitated and then responded, "Right."

"And you and Pat are best friends, right?"

Carol's face had a strange expression on it as if she didn't know where Sandy was going with this, but she said, "Right."

"I think this story is so great." Sandy was bubbling over with excitement. "I have never heard of two women being such good friends after being married to the same man. What is so great is that you don't refer to each other as my ex-husband's wife. But you call each other best friends! Ken and I talk about this and we'd love to hear the story about how this came about. You know, you two should write a book."

Back at home Carol and I talked about what Sandy had said. "What do you think has been the key thing in our friendship?" I asked Carol.

"Oh, Pat, I think it all goes back to when you and David made a conscious decision that you would be friends. I know in the beginning it was for the boys' sake. Both of us feel it has made things easier for the whole family. You saw it yourself on Thanksgiving when we were here with you and Gary and two of the boys. We've shared so many family events together, haven't we? Christmas holidays, birthdays, graduations, weddings. And it's not just David and I attending his boys' stuff. It's the whole family being at parties involving my John. All three of the boys were groomsmen at John and Chris' wedding, and you and Gary and your mother attended. You know my John considers you his step-mom."

I chuckled, "Yeah, they even come to see us in Florida without you! I think that David and I staying friends is part of it. But a big part of what makes our relationship work is that you and Gary are willing to accept the friendship David and I have. Most spouses would not allow it, let alone go along with it."

I thought of how I spent four months up north working with our son Mark in the housing business and also with David in his home improvement work. I looked at my friend and thought how some days Carol would send David and me on our way to work without an ounce of hesitation. She trusted us.

Gary considered us all friends and was glad I could be working with our son as well as David. Definitely, Gary and Carol's willingness played a very important part in our unusual friendship. The two of them had to look deep inside themselves to see if they could take on a friendship that potentially might not be the best for them or for us.

But they took on the friendship, and it has been a gift from God. We have been the best of friends for over thirty years, and we care deeply for each other. All four of the boys and Gary's two kids were OK with our friendship, even though it was probably easier on them before David and I remarried.

David and Carol were married in June of 1979. Gary and I married in December of 1979. The boys probably thought each couple would have their separate lives. I am sure they were pleasantly surprised. I know my boys liked Carol from the beginning, and Carol's son John warmed up to me. The boys' spouses may have at times questioned the whole one-big-happy-family thing. Now we're accustomed to it and enjoy the fun and laughter we have together. Gary's two children, Greg and Vickie, at times thought it strange. But once they got to know everyone, they seemed to love their new brothers. The same goes for their three brothers. Our lives just went on.

I looked over at my friend Carol. We have such different personalities, but we both have a sense of humor. I'm more outspoken than she is. She is one of a kind—a treasure. She was put here in this space and time to save a very close friend's life—David. From the first time I met her, I thought she had a wonderful way about her. I thought about the way she shares her smile and the way it lights up the room. She has a big heart and a good, sensitive soul. She loves the Lord. She knows that life doesn't always play by the rules, but that in the long run everything will work out. She loves to shop. You will never see her without everything matching—right down to her shoes and jewelry. And she lets me be me with no strings attached. It's an unconditional friendship. I thank God for giving me the treasure of our friendship.

Chapter 7

EVERY CLOUD HAS A SILVER LINING
(OR IS THAT ALUMINUM?)

Carol

I wandered outside and sat down in the sun to take a little break from packing. Leaning back on a deck chair, I relaxed and let the memories swirl around me. Good memories they were too. I thought about that special night when I met my dreamboat. October 22, 1976. You never meet the right guy in a bar, or so I thought. That night was different. I had gone to the Point After Nightclub right after work with my co-worker and friend, Elsa. We were having a few drinks and I was on this kick of asking people, "What's your story?" Then I spotted this tall, handsome guy in the three-piece plaid suit.

"This guy has to be an attorney," I told Elsa. "I'd love to meet him." I just *had* to meet him. After staring at him for what seemed forever as he leaned against the wall, I got up and went up to the bar to get another drink. As I walked back to our table, something strongly impressed me to turn and look back. When I did, my eyes locked with his. He motioned with his index finger for me to come over to him. Even though I thought I was one of those play-hard-to-get girls, I did a 180-degree speed turn and marched right over to meet him.

Ours was a whirlwind courtship. We saw each other every day after that for a couple of months. The night after we met he took me to his mother's birthday party at his sister's house. His family thought we had known each other for a while. I was too embarrassed to tell them we had just met the night before! I wasn't that kind of girl, you know. Before we went to his sister's, we had to stop to see his boys at his ex-wife's house. I was a little nervous because I hadn't dated anyone with an ex-wife so close by. In fact, I had never dated someone who wanted to take me to his ex-wife's house!

I asked David about his relationship with the mother of his sons. When he explained how they had remained friends through the years even though they had divorced and he remarried again I was intrigued. I remember thinking this was pretty cool, but strange. I didn't know then that I would learn over the years just how strange it was to the outside world.

The night I met Pat, I liked her immediately. She had a way of making you laugh and making everyone around her feel comfortable.

David and I dated regularly over the next year and a half. I found out the night I met him that he wasn't an attorney, but he owned a home improvement company. I had never known anyone in this line of work so it was a learning experience. He was exciting to be with, strong yet gentle. I worked at the capitol building for a state senator, so we met almost every day for lunch downtown. David sure knew how to court a girl. He sent me flowers and always planned something fun to do.

Right away I met his three teenage sons and introduced them to my seven-year-old son. David's mom, dad and siblings were a very loving, hugging family and they welcomed me with open arms. He took me up north to the cottage he was building at Bear Lake. This place nestled on a hill in the woods came to be our weekend refuge.

That year and a half of dating went by quickly with very few bumps in the road of our relationship.

I didn't see Pat much during that time. David's boys went up north with us every other weekend—mandatory—so we stopped and picked them up on those Fridays. I knew David would go over there or call every day, but that was fine with me. That's one of the things I loved about him—he loved to spend time with his family. I could tell that he and Pat were good friends. When they were together they'd joke around and enjoy each other's company. He cared about and watched over his children's mother and tried to help out whenever he was asked.

My ex, John, Sr., and I had also remained friends. We didn't talk to each other every day, but we were nevertheless friends. I know he found David and my relationship with Pat unusual.

The day I knew Pat was a special woman is when I asked her if I could have a surprise birthday party for David's thirty-ninth at her house. That took nerve, but I didn't have enough room at my apartment for all the family and friends. Thinking back now I can't believe I asked her that. I guess I believed she and David really were friends. She said yes, and we had a great party with family, friends, music, drinking and dancing.

Not too much was said among us about Betty—old number two. I did meet her and got reports from the family that nobody ever liked her. It sounded like she and David had been in an emotional, short and volatile relationship. I knew David still saw her once in a while when he would disappear for a whole day and be out of contact with everybody, including me. We had no commitment then, so I had my "little secret times" too!

Eventually, David and I became more committed to each other. He moved in with John and me in Haslett. At the time, I never thought about the moral messages we were sending to his kids and mine. Besides, I thought I was a good person. I was definitely not religious. I had been to Sunday school a little bit as a young girl but that was it. That was just about to change.

Chapter 8

OUR UMBRELLA IS UP

CAROL

In the Bear Lake Township where David's cottage was, there was a little community church where his Uncle Glenn was the preacher. David and I began attending the services. I don't remember if Uncle Glenn was a good preacher or not. But he was so full of love that it overflowed out of him and into anyone standing close enough to feel it.

January 21, 1978, we stopped by to visit his aunt and uncle. We had a few questions about what we had heard in church about being "born again." Neither of us had any thought of putting aside our worldly natures that day; we were just curious. Uncle Glenn and Aunt Lila talked to us for a long time and finally Aunt Lila said, "You know today is the day of salvation."

David and I didn't have time to talk and consult each other about this. This was a personal and individual decision. Without each other knowing it, we both decided in our hearts to accept Jesus as Savior into our lives. I thought I was a good person and my life was great before then, but I hadn't done too well with relationships, so why not?

David and I knelt in Uncle Glenn and Aunt Lila's living room. We both asked Christ into our lives and to forgive us of all our sins. For all our years without Christ there was a lot to forgive. But we believed that He did.

I was excited about sharing what happened with my co-workers on Monday. First thing I asked them, "Guess what David and I did this weekend?" Of course, they couldn't have guessed in a million years. Finally I said, "We got saved!"

"Saved from what?" was their honest response. So, as a baby Christian, I tried to explain that I was a sinner and needed to be saved. They quickly came to my defense, telling me what a wonderful, good person I was. I decided I was not qualified to explain all this, as I didn't understand it myself. I just knew what had happened to us.

David and I started reading the Bible together as often as we could. We read at home. As we drove up north and back we found it was a good reading time. David would read out loud and I would drive. We wanted to get to know this forgiving God a lot better.

Our lives changed dramatically.

David's boys sat back and waited to see how long this would last.

One of the first changes in our lives became evident as we began wondering if we should be living together. We had been reading and studying the Bible. We took in as much as we possibly could—classes at a local Bible college and many seminars. This went on for about a year. One day God used a bad snowstorm and the word "fornication" in the Bible passage we were reading to get our attention. We realized that we needed to either get married or separate. This opened a can of worms because David was gun-shy about tying the knot again. In the world, it's three strikes and you're out!

We decided to separate. For three months we did not see each other. For me it was agony. But God used that to show me who the most important person in my life should be, even before my family. I finally learned that I did not have to have a man in my life. What I really needed was God in my life. My priorities changed. First it was God, then my son John, and then my family. I still got lonely without someone right there "in person" to share my life with besides my son. But God knew the desires of my heart.

I missed the friends David and I knew "up north," so John and I went up for the weekend in April. I loved my friend's place on Bear Lake. I enjoyed sitting on their swing and just watching the water. They had three kids, and John and their son had a good time playing together. I had time to think and reflect. I came to the conclusion, after being separated from David for what seemed like an eternity, that I didn't want to continue being apart from him.

Back at home we talked and both agreed we did not like life apart from each other. But David certainly didn't want to get married unless God told him he could. I had been reading about Queen Esther in the Bible who fasted. We decided then and there that we would fast for three days and pray that God would show David if he should marry me or not. On the third day we would get together to see what the answer was.

Those were the longest days. I fasted and drank water for three days—no coffee, juice or food—just water. I did a lot of praying. Mainly I asked God, "How in the world are you going to make him listen to your voice? How are you going to get the message across to him?" I couldn't imagine it. I thought God would have to write a physical letter and drop it in his mailbox.

On the third day he called in the afternoon to see if I could come to his office. Of course I could. I left work early, a little anxious. When I arrived, he ushered me into his office and had me sit down across from him. It was so good to see him. I had missed him so much those three months.

"What kind of a fast did we agree on?" he asked me.

"I don't think we agreed on a specific kind," I said, puzzled.

David continued questioning me on what kind of fast we had agreed upon. I couldn't remember that we had set any guidelines.

"Exactly how did you fast?" he asked. "Did you have coffee with the girls?"

Wondering what he was getting at I tried to assure him. "No, I only drank water," I said. "Not even any breath mints or gum."

David pulled out a piece of paper, unfolded it and began reading what God had told him.

I thought, *God did write him a letter!* The letter was to me. During David's three-day fast God showed him that it was important how I fasted. If I fasted with juice and other liquids, it meant I was a wonderful woman but not the one for David to marry. If, on the other hand, I had fasted with water only that meant I was strong and committed and I was the one David could marry.

"Well, praise the Lord!" I said. I about jumped across the desk and into his lap. Oh happy day! To say I was excited was an understatement.

We set a June wedding date, which was a little over a month away. I was on a cloud and started making wedding plans immediately.

We were married at Bear Lake Christian, the summer church services which Uncle Glenn held at the Bear Lake Township Hall. Our wedding was part of the service. David and I walked down the aisle at the end of the service when everyone was expecting the closing hymn. Instead, they got to witness a wedding. My mom stood up for me. All of our boys stood up for David. Our reception was at our friend's home on Bear Lake. The setting was beautiful and the catered meal delicious. And so our life together with God began.

Just after our wedding we heard that Pat had been dating a man she met at her office. Of course, David needed to check this guy out and give Pat the OK. She probably wouldn't have listened if he hadn't approved! We both liked Gary from the start and were pleased when they announced wedding plans for December. We attended the wedding, as did many of David's family. By June 1980 they were off to New York City, where Gary had been accepted at the General Theological Seminary. His desire was to become an Episcopal priest.

The sun had moved behind a cloud and it was time to get inside and help Pat. As I got up I thought about the roads of our lives that met and crossed again and again. It was all because of this unique friendship with my husband's first wife. It does seem strange to others, but God can do what we think is unthinkable or impossible. I thought about how much we had been through together. We had seen sickness—David's cancer. There had been deaths, weddings, divorces, celebrations, prosperity and lean times.

I thought about what a strong person Pat is. She is committed to her family and her friends. She's always ready to help them whenever and however she can. She can make you laugh when there's nothing to laugh about. Her sense of humor brings joy to everyone around her. She's a good listener if you need to unload. She gives good advice to help you get through any situation. She loves God and knows that she and Gary have a calling on their lives. She has helped me through some hard times in my life. I can't think of a time now or in the future when we wouldn't be friends. We're friends forever, just as Michael W. Smith talks about in his song.

"This is it." Pat came down from upstairs, declaring she was done packing for today. "I can hardly get through those books without all those old memories cropping up."

"Me too," I smiled.

As we talked about some of the times we had shared, I asked Pat, "What do we do now?"

Pat quickly responded, "Let's write a book."

I said, "Let's talk about it."

Just then the phone rang. It was David. I put him on the speakerphone and away he went, talking about his day. When he finished I said, "Write it down. We'll put it in the book!"

Chapter 9

WHO NEEDS AN UMBRELLA?

DAVID

I was sitting in the breakfast nook working on my sermon for Sunday, when and my mind started to wander. I was waiting for a call from Carol's father's doctor. I wanted to bring him in to see the doctor as he wasn't doing well. He couldn't stand up by himself; he was so weak. I hoped to get him in and treated without having to call Carol home from St. Louis. She was out there helping her best friend (and my first wife) Pat pack and get ready to move. Gary had gotten another church in Florida and it looked like that is where they were going to settle. I was distracted from my work on my sermon and sat staring out into the pond and our beautiful garden. The blossoms were bright this time of year. I really enjoyed working in the garden. I chuckled to myself thinking thirty years ago I would have thought someone was loony if he told me I would be gardening in my middle age. Many things have changed from those days. I, especially, have changed. Thank God.

Isn't life strange? Here I am married to my third wife, Carol. It's amazing that once I turned my life over to God, He gave me a third chance to be the kind of husband He wanted me to be. He knew I never wanted to marry any of my wives. I just wasn't the marrying type. So now my third wife is helping my first wife Pat move. They have become best friends, and they didn't even know each other until I met Carol and took her over to meet Pat. God does have a sense of humor, doesn't He?

I was sixteen years old when I met my first love, a wonderful, beautiful young girl, Patricia Powell. I went with her for approximately five years. Not being able to take a relationship seriously, I was unfaithful throughout this relationship.

I loved her, but I don't know if we would have married if our first son, Mark, hadn't been conceived. In those days, you did what you should do under the circumstances, so we got married. Once you were married you were supposed to stay married. Two more sons later, I still wasn't becoming a better husband. I was definitely not mature enough for this relationship. By then the devil had such a death grip on me, he controlled just about everything in my life, and my unfaithfulness continued.

My love for Pat grew along with my frustration with life. I didn't seem to fit in anywhere. Why? I have no defense for the way I lived. We all want to have somebody or something to blame—I have neither. Most of my affairs were one-night stands. I had a restless, wayward spirit that did not allow me to settle down. But I was happy with Pat as a wife and as a mother to my children. I loved my family and was very close to them.

I had wonderful parents and was brought up in a good family. There were two half-brothers who didn't live with us, Arnold and Francis. I had two half-sisters who did live with us, Donna Lou and Joyce. Then there was my older sister Charlene and two younger brothers, Dick and Gordon.

My father and mother were not drinkers, or partying people. They weren't abusive in any way. They were Christians. We were brought up in a good, sound, Bible-believing church—the United Brethren Church in Lansing, Michigan. My Aunt Lila was my Sunday school teacher. I believed all I was taught and always have.

So how does a person get so far off track? How does he so desperately lose his way? I trace it back to peer pressure—making the wrong choices for my friends.

As a very young boy I was sexually abused by an older cousin and also by an older boy in our neighborhood. This messed me up for quite a while. I have never held any hatred or unforgiveness towards my violators. No one else knows who they are and I see no reason for anyone to ever know. However, this did sexually disorient me for a while. I am not suggesting that any of these things are to blame for my twenty-five years of torment. But these experiences can make a child growing up jump track.

Of the eight children, I was the least attractive. Well-meaning relatives never ceased to wonder out loud, "What happened to David?" I was very skinny and through remarks made by relatives and friends, I became very self-conscious and tried to cover it up. I even secretly bought a product called Weight-On by mail order. Unfortunately, I was never able to add weight. I even sought the mail order help of Charles Atlas with no results.

As a young teenager, I tried hard to be accepted by my peers. My cousin informed me that girls don't like boys with red hair and freckles. I had red hair and freckles. Oh great, I thought, what am I doing here anyway? Then suddenly my freckles were masked by a very bad case of acne, then a plague of boils and carbuncles. This kept me out of sports, which I loved. My folks were wonderful, but they had no idea what I was going through. We didn't talk about things much back then.

I started running with hoodlums. They seemed to accept me regardless of my physical shortcomings. For us it was all about drinking, getting high, and partying. As I became an older teenager, I learned that other partiers weren't quite so particular about what you looked like as long as you were into having fun, and willing to do about anything they wanted to do.

When I became a husband and a father it was hard to lose those hoodlum traits. I loved to party. Pat and I had many parties at our house. I partied at home and away from home, still trying to find something, but I didn't know what it was. I loved being home with my kids but I was always drawn away. The business I was in didn't help. Being in sales can give you lots of excuses to be away from home.

Then something happened I didn't expect. I fell in love and/or lust with a woman who I worked with in real estate. She was a beautiful, wonderful lady who just happened to be unhappily married. The commitments of marriage, family and togetherness did not compute with me. Now, I could relate to business. Betty was a sales agent like me so we hit it off immediately. I was an avid hunter and loved to go deer hunting, bear hunting, and duck hunting. I guess I was the same in my life. The chase and the hunt seemed to be my excitement, but I never really wanted to catch the game.

I had a wonderful wife and three sons at home, whom I loved dearly. My running around didn't seem to have anything to do with that part of my life, but little did I know that it really did. I would not hurt any of my loved ones on purpose. I really did love my family. You know what Flip Wilson always said, "The devil made me do it." I am not trying to make excuses and avoid taking responsibility, but there was something during that time that I had no control over—my lust.

The bottom line to it all was Pat and I divorced, and Betty became my second wife. I still didn't want to be married. I was miserable living with her and miserable living without her, so I decided to try it with her. It was a year's emotional roller-coaster ride. She had one son and I had my three boys every other weekend. I tried hard to please everyone. When Betty asked me to choose her over my boys we separated and divorced. To me there was no reason that I had to choose, but she insisted, so I chose.

After that, I poured all my energies into my boys. Pat and I had chosen to stay good friends and am I glad.

It was just before my divorce was final with Betty in 1977 that I met Carol at the Point After Bar in downtown Lansing. She worked at the capitol, and I had my home improvement business. After our first meeting, we saw each other almost every day. I took her to my mother's birthday party on our second date and over to meet Pat and the boys that same night. I wondered what Carol was thinking. She had one son, John, who was much younger than my sons. Her ex lived right in Lansing and also worked at the capitol. My family liked her immediately and she seemed to fit into my life. We had a lot of fun times, but marriage never entered into my thoughts, even after we moved in together. We lived in our apartment during the week, and went up north every weekend, as I loved getting out in nature in northern Michigan. Almost every day we had lunch together and just enjoyed being with each other.

Thinking back on it now, I know that God loved me and had His hand on my life. He protected me but let me run right to the end of my chain. I had tried hard early in life to become a hoodlum, but I never really fit in aside from my infidelity problem. I was honest in all other ways, responsible, considerate of others, and always paid my debts. I never hurt another person in any way.

Alcohol was an unfamiliar spirit in my family. I never saw my parents, grandparents, aunts or uncles drink. Usually this type of addiction runs in families. I recently figured out why I started drinking. With all the negatives in my life growing up—being skinny, with my red hair, freckles, pimples, and boils, I had a real inferiority complex.

The spirit that did run in my family was a whoremonger demon. Infidelity ran in my family, alcohol and drugs didn't. I worked hard to become a drunk and relied on other drugs to get me where I wanted to be. My life was a mess. I was shy and introverted, but learned that after five to six beers I had the courage to confront women with a boldness that won their attention. I had a gentle, loving spirit, so this wasn't what I really wanted in my life. But it seemed to work for me. I wasn't your typical falling-down drunk type who would go on two- or three-day binges. I was a functional drunk, never missing work as the result of drinking. Nevertheless, I was drunk three to five times a week, partying my way through two families.

After so many years, I grew weary. Nothing was working in my life. I made good money, lived the high-rolling lifestyle, yet I wasn't content. So, I just kept running. Finally at the end of my chain, I went out looking for help.

New Year's Eve 1977 I was drunk, partying at the cottage in Kalkaska. I called my dad to wish him "Happy New Year." I shouldn't have called, but I loved my mom and dad and it seemed proper to call them. When my dad answered the phone, I wished him, "Happy New Year," chit-chatted a while, then asked him, "Did you make any New Year's resolutions, Dad?"

"Nope."

This puzzled me since I always made many and never kept any.

"Why not?"

"I didn't need to."

Without me being aware of it, his answer started working subconsciously on me. During the next three weeks, Carol and I attended the People's Church in Kalkaska. My Uncle Glenn was the interim pastor there for the winter, as Bear Lake Church was just a summer church. Three Sundays in a row, this strange feeling came over me when they sang the last song and had an altar call. My thoughts went something like this: *What's going on? This will surely hamper my lifestyle. I've got to get out of here.*

One Saturday morning Carol and I found ourselves going over to Uncle Glenn and Aunt Lila's. It was January 21, 1978, to be exact. Our idea was to get more information so someday we could get saved, but not now. I had more partying to do and fun to have. But as we talked, everything they were saying sounded so good, just like I wanted my life to be. They talked about the peace and joy that I had forfeited for the past twenty-five years. The ole devil spoke to me and reminded me of all the hypocrites out there, saying, "You don't want to be like them." He was right. I'm an honest man, I thought, and I couldn't profess one lifestyle and live another.

Then my Aunt Lila spoke the Word, "Today is the day of salvation." I thought, *I don't want it to be today. I've got to get out of here!* Then the Lord spoke to me saying, "David, let me worry about the hypocrites. The only shoes you have to stand in on Judgment Day are yours." Although I wanted to leave, I suddenly thought, *I really do believe in Heaven and Hell, and I really want to spend eternity in Heaven. What if I leave here and get killed in a car accident?*

My life was like a five-hundred-piece jigsaw puzzle. Every time I would get it almost together and looking pretty good, I would come up a piece short and it was never complete. Jesus was the missing piece. He said, "Come unto me all you who are weary and heavy laden and I will give you rest."

Carol and I and Uncle Glenn and Aunt Lila got on our knees around their coffee table. Uncle Glenn led us in a sinner's prayer. We repented of our sins and invited Jesus into our lives.

Talk about a change in lifestyles! Before Christ I smoked two packs of cigarettes per day. After Christ, in twenty-eight years I have never had an urge to do so. Before Christ I drank three to five nights a week. After Christ I haven't been drunk or abused drugs in twenty-eight years. Before Christ I committed adultery hundreds of times. After Christ I have never committed adultery. Before Christ I went to two to three wild parties a week. After Christ no wild parties. Before Christ I spent all my money on my low lifestyle. After Christ, for twenty-eight years,

I have invested wisely. I am a changed man. To this day I thank the Lord for not giving up on me.

Three months after our born-again experience, Carol and I were blessed to go to Florida with my mother and father and Uncle Glenn and Aunt Lila. We spent two weeks at a Christian retreat in Bradenton, going to church three times a day, growing in the Lord and loving it. It was there in April of 1978 we received the baptism of the Holy Spirit.

After months of living together, God had us separate for a season. We were married in June of 1979. That is a miracle in itself because I still never wanted to be married. But now I wanted to be a man after God's own heart. After Carol and I fasted for three days, God revealed to me very clearly that I could marry Carol. We were married at the end of a church service at Bear Lake Christian Church with Carol's mom standing up for her and my three boys, Mark, Matt, Mitch and Carol's son John standing up for me. The whole congregation witnessed it. We still run into people who talk about our wedding.

I had gone through thirteen years of school and never studied a book or paid attention in class. At forty years of age I started attending every Bible class I could. I attended two different Bible colleges over a three-year period. I attended a Billy Graham Bible seminar in Toronto with Carol. I went from hating teachers to becoming a teacher. I now love to study.

We did missionary work in Guatemala, Central America, from 1985 to 1996. I went down there one to two times a year. On two occasions, Carol and I drove old school buses down, loaded with supplies, with our Christian friends, Ray and Esther Garza. We bought property in Los Margueritas, just outside Guatemala City, and built a small church and school. We worked with a bilingual Guatemalan, Abraham Yol Boro. The first trip was with evangelist and friend, Kennard Van Camp, and I made several trips with him over the years.

Our lives were changed. But, my hardest trial was yet to come.

Chapter 10

I KNEW, THAT I KNEW, THAT I KNEW

DAVID

In March of 1991, I discovered a large lump growing on the left side of my neck. There was no pain, so I wasn't too concerned about it.

My company was doing a siding job for a lady who worked at a cancer clinic. Knowing she worked with cancer patients, I casually told her about the lump on my neck. Until then I hadn't considered that it might be cancer.

She had a look, and said she couldn't be sure, but advised strongly that I see a doctor and have it checked. When I made an appointment with the doctor I thought it was waste of money—but I did it anyway. The doctor thought it was cancer, but he needed to get a biopsy. After three biopsies, three pathologists diagnosed me with squamous cell carcinoma—a cancer that can be caused by smoking. I had not smoked for twelve years. I had smoked for twenty-five years before I quit. But this cancer can happen up to fifteen years after you quit. I was stunned!

I didn't want to have cancer. I didn't want to go through what I had seen so many friends and relatives go through. I was too busy. I also didn't want to die. Spiritually, I was ready to die, but emotionally I wasn't ready. I had loved ones I wanted to see get saved, grandkids to see grow up, things I wanted to do, and work that needed to be done.

Our son Mark went with Carol and me to our doctor appointment to discuss the options. The doctor said I would need chemotherapy. I had recently seen my brother-in-law sick and weak from taking chemo, and after a few months he died anyway. Everyone I had seen take chemo died after being very sick the last few months of their lives. I didn't like this option. The doctor also said I needed to get started with thirty-five radiation treatments, one per day, five days a week, for seven weeks. If I did all of this, he only gave me a 40/60 percent chance to live. I am not a gambler, and I didn't like those odds.

I'd wake up in the middle of the night, stare at the ceiling, cry and wonder, *Why me?* I couldn't believe this was happening. After my pity parties were over, we commenced to pray. We learned that to get results in prayer we needed to only have people of faith, who believe God still answers prayers and who believe in miracles, praying for us. I also learned it was important to purge any sin from your life, especially the sin of unforgiveness.

Denny Freeman was the pastor at Bear Lake Christian Church at the time. He was a man of God who believed that God performed miracles and answered prayer. He was also elder/associate pastor of the Gaylord Community Church. We first had our people at Bear Lake Christian Church pray for my healing. We went to Gaylord Community Church and asked them to pray. Then we went to Dr. Lanny Johnson's Bible study at his office in Okemos, Michigan. They prayed for me, and Lanny specifically prayed for God to activate my immune system to take care of the cancer cells. We went to Harbor Light Church in Harbor Springs, Michigan, and went up for prayer at the altar. We had people from Fenton come up who were part of Harvest House, as well as Pastor Kennard Van Camp, our dear friend and brother in the Lord for many years. These friends had seen many healings in their ministry. They came to the halfway house we had going for men at our farmhouse on M-72 and spent much time with Carol and me, counseling us and helping us get our hearts clean.

Then, it was time for me to make some decisions. I knew God healed miraculously and I knew He also heals through doctors. I thought constantly of what to do. Should I do the chemo and the radiation? The doctors recommended both.

I took my dog, Sissy, and spent twenty-four hours in my hunting shack fasting and praying. I believe the Lord put on my heart not to do the chemo. My doctor was disappointed, but honored my decision. I felt I was to do the radiation. When I went in to start treatment they tattooed my neck in three places, to line up their machine exactly each time. The thought of thirty-five trips to Traverse City, Michigan, over the next seven weeks didn't excite me. I dreaded starting my scheduled appointments in two weeks, but knew we needed to get on with it.

Early one Sunday morning in late March the Lord woke me up and told me to go to the prayer house. Now, my prayer house is an outbuilding. It was very cold outside and I was very comfortable snuggled up to my wife. I said, "Yes, Lord, as soon as it's time to get up and it warms up a little I'll come right out to meet You." I went back to sleep. He woke me up again. This time He got my full attention. I got up, dressed and headed for the prayer house. It was still dark and very cold outside. I entered my prayer house and lit some candles and got down on my face before the Lord. The devil came to me first. He knew I didn't want to die and figured I would do anything not to. The devil told me, "If you come back to my world, I will heal you." Immediately I rebuked him in the name of Jesus. He fled, and then God came to me. He said, "I am going to heal you." He didn't say how or when, but from that point on I never again had the fear that I had known throughout this ordeal.

I was already tattooed for the radiation treatments. I figured if the healing was manifested before the treatment started, I would cancel the treatments. It hadn't and I didn't. So I believed that God would heal me through the treatments. The big day came. We drove to Traverse City and started the radiation treatments. Five or six days went by. I thought—no problem, this is a piece of cake. By the tenth day it was quite a different story. My throat was burned badly. I mentioned this to the doctor. Without checking it, he commented that he knew it would happen because they were hitting me with over a million volts of radiation to this area.

I went back for day eleven, day twelve, and day thirteen, and day fourteen. At this point, I told the doctor to check my throat. My throat was burned so badly I couldn't even swallow my saliva. His comment was, "Wow!" He sent me back to my ear, nose and throat doctor. When he checked, he said he had never seen anything like it before. He was so amazed he even had Carol look at it. She said it looked burned and swollen shut. He called the radiation clinic and told them to discontinue the treatment for a week. That was a Thursday. On Sunday I gave an unspoken prayer request. No one knew what it was. I felt it had to be that way.

On the Friday before, a Christian inmate had called from the Muskegon Correctional Facility. I wasn't home, but Carol talked to him and told him of my situation, and he assured her he would be in prayer. Carol forgot to tell me that he had called. On Tuesday I received a letter from him and it started out like this: "Brother David and Sister Carol, since Carol told me about your throat on Friday, I've been praying in the Spirit. The reason your throat is burned so badly is because God had already healed you! And the radiation is destructive."

My silent prayer that last Sunday had been: "Father would You speak to me about Your healing through someone, so that I will know if I should continue with the radiation treatments?"

After receiving the letter from Bill Burke, I knew it was a direct answer to the silent prayer that no one had known about, except God and me. I knew, that I knew, that I knew, that God had healed me.

I made an appointment with the radiation doctor at the clinic and discussed with him what had happened over the past week since he stopped the treatments. The treatments were due to start back up, and I had twenty-one more to go. I explained to him that I wouldn't be taking the rest of the treatments because God had healed me. He was a Christian, and he said he believed that God healed people, but that God gave some people brains to be doctors and medical people and He healed through them. He asked me to talk to the senior pastor at Faith Reformed Church in Traverse City.

Carol and I made an appointment and spoke to the pastor. We shared our faith in this matter and the story of God's healing. He also shared his belief in miracle healing as well as healing through doctors. He knew our minds were not going to be changed so he prayed with us and sent us on our way.

I made another appointment with my radiation doctor. Carol and I shared with him about our meeting with the pastor and told him we appreciated all that he had done as well as his feelings about this. We really loved and appreciated the concern and tender heart of this young doctor. But our minds were not changed. I would be discontinuing the treatments. He wept, as he knew this was our final decision and nothing would change our minds. He gently pleaded with us saying, "But, you will surely die."

For a testimony, I agreed to go in every month for the first year and quarterly for the next two years so they could monitor what was going on. I never heard verbal praise to the Lord from them, but I have often wondered how God used this with them.

It's been about thirteen years since then. I give the praise and glory to God. I certainly don't speak smugly about this, as it was nothing I did. God did it and I give Him all the glory and praise. Thank you, Abba Father!

My sister, Charlene, who was diagnosed with cancer shortly after me, fought it hard for three years. Her faith was great. She hadn't lived the kind of life I had during my twenty-five years of running from the Lord. I was sure God was going to raise her up even in her last days, but she went to be with the Lord. For three days afterwards, until her funeral, I was perplexed. I didn't understand why she didn't experience healing.

God showed me that for a Christian who is ready to go and be with the Lord, death is the ultimate healing. "Precious in the sight of the Lord is the death of his saints." My healing was secondary. It's difficult for us to get a grip on this. Our Father's ways are not ours and I know my sister is safe in the care of our Lord Jesus Christ.

It was after I was healed from cancer that I received the call to become the pastor of Bear Lake Christian Church in September of 1992. Carol and I have been pastoring the church since that time and love the work our Lord has called us to.

Carol and I and Pat and Gary have been very close friends, taking trips and spending holidays together. It all seems so incredible—Pat is married to a priest and I became a pastor.

Chapter 11

THE RIBS THAT HOLD THE UMBRELLA UP

Pat & Carol

Sharing our families was a thread that held our friendship together. Carol and I talked on the phone at least once a week. It only took a few hours of talking on the phone to catch up. This was especially important when we all lived far away from each other. When any of our children—and it never mattered which child from which parent—had a problem we'd talk. We'd share the problem with each other and try to decide what we could do to help. That is what mothers and grandmothers do. For as long as we have been friends, we have shared our joys and tears. The guys could never understand how we could talk so long. We had plenty to talk about. We'd share with each other what the kids and the grandchildren did from day one. We'd share their ups and downs—and there have been many. Together as couples, we have seventeen grandchildren and four great-grandchildren. I always felt bad that I couldn't see them often and hold them and watch them grow into such fine adults. Now they call and keep in touch.

Carol knew I felt bad about being away as the grandkids grew up. But when you go into the ministry, you have to go where God leads you. Carol always felt fortunate that she and David were able to stay in one area so they had a lot of time with the kids and grandkids. I stayed connected with the family through my long phone conversations with Carol. She would relay everything that was going on.

Through the years, Gary and I ended up in a Michigan church off and on. Then we could see the family more. Both Mitch and John live in Florida where Gary and I are now. All of us love it when the family can get together, whether in Florida or Michigan. When we share our families with each other the bonds are strengthened between the whole family, not just us. Not many couples or friends are able to do that.

There is another tie that binds us together. We have in each other someone to talk to about the sometimes high-stress career of being clergy spouses. Many others have written about this subject, so I won't say much. Carol and I both agree that the biggest complaint we hear from other clergy spouses is that they wish they had a real friend they could share all of their mixed up moments and confused thoughts with—someone to laugh and cry with. So many women have had to learn the hard way and probably some have not even made it through.

Carol and I have many stories we share with each other. The churches Gary and David serve are very different. One is more formal and the other more relaxed and laid back. We both have been through hard church times. But instead of the loneliness so many clergy wives experience, we've had each other to talk things over with. We've had someone who understands what the other is going through on an average Sunday. We understand each other, that we can't be, and don't want to be, perfect. We both know that neither of us is perfect. We all need to be accepted for who we really are. We could list each other's imperfections, but they don't matter. That's what I call a perfect friendship!

Most church members are afraid to get too close to us as pastors' wives. And sometimes it is scary for us to get too close to church members. Both of us have experienced pain in this area. There certainly are exceptions to the rule, but generally a pastor's wife has to be very careful for her husband's sake. Only other clergy wives understand that they have to show up at most church functions, while their church friends can have an abundance of good excuses. A clergy wife has to be on the brink of death to miss something at church. There is also the Saturday night out "no-no." People do things on Saturday night. That is hard for a minister because he is usually preparing for Sunday. If you do get to go to a dinner or get-together, you will probably have to leave earlier than anyone else. That is part of being in the ministry.

At one parish where we served, one of the women of the church and I had an interesting conversation. From the comments she made I knew she assumed that I fit the "clergy spouse" pattern she had in her head. After that conversation was over, the lady never did talk to me again. Some people cannot accept you as real. They want you to be what they want you to be.

Carol told me when David first became the pastor of their church, she was quick to let it be known that she didn't play the piano or take care of children's church. Those functions seem to be the typical job description for a pastor's wife. Of course David didn't sing either.

I laugh when I remember when someone introduced me by saying, "This is Pat." The other person said, "Hello." Then the person who introduced me said, "Pat is the priest's wife." From the other person's reaction, all of a sudden I had turned into someone who was famous. I thought, *What about the real me? What happened to Pat?*

It's often said our life is like a fishbowl, open for whoever wants to see in. In a sense that is true. I know in my position as a pastor's wife it's important for me to live an exemplary lifestyle.

Unfortunately, because I am human, that is not always easy to do. Should I have that one glass of wine or will that offend someone? Can I watch my favorite sitcom on TV? If someone in the church finds out, will he or she think I am unspiritual? What about drinking that favorite cup of coffee, or spending money when some of our people don't have any? These are hard questions. I try to keep in mind that the Bible says not to be a stumbling block and that helps me answer these questions.

I do love our parishes. But if there is any sacrifice, it's that we have been away from our family as a result of moving so much. Our personal lives have been shared with the church.

Carol and David have been in the same church, along with their family, since 1979. They actually grew up spiritually in this church so sometimes it is easy for them to be taken for granted. But they wouldn't be where they are if it wasn't for faithful people holding them up and praying for them, supporting them in many ways.

We both have learned very quickly that a sense of humor is essential to surviving the peculiar stress and strains of life in the church. Oh, there is always the big question of how it is to live with a man who is so holy and perfect! What his admiring parishioners don't know is that at home this quality sometimes humanizes itself to a point where it borders on the catatonic. When Gary comes in after I have eaten dinner by myself and I'm waiting to tell him about my day, all I want is his attention. He has had a day of long meetings, hospital calls, and dealing with people with problems. It's no wonder that he doesn't have much left for his wife.

But Carol and I agree that we have happy marriages and thank God for that. We both think it has been easier for us because neither of us have children living at home. One clergy wife shared with me about the toll of a divorce in her life. She said, "Every time I prayed I would see the vision of a back door. Finally, one day I went through it." Think about it—a divorce in a clergy home is a lot different from that in a "normal home," if there is such a thing. We must remember that even though these guys are holy, they are also human.

The greatest joy of being a clergy wife? Hmm, let's see. Well, both Carol and I agree we love to listen to our husband's sermons…especially the endings.

It's that sense of humor you must keep at all times!

Another important thing you must have is an open door of communication. Some people ask if we get jealous of the other women involved in the ministry with our husbands. That can sometimes be a problem if things aren't kept in the open. In David and Carol's church, they have a woman counselor, so most of the women who need help can talk with her or both her and the pastor. The bottom line is we all have to answer to God.

I love what Henri Nouwen says—that participating in the church is the most important discipline in developing one's spiritual life. Yet for clergy spouses the very church they love and which nurtures them is also that which can cause pain and stress. Ambivalent feelings toward the church are understandable but still distressing. Perhaps, by acknowledging these feelings and understanding them better, we can reduce our sense of isolation and guilt and prevent these feelings from festering into a destructive relationship. This would be beneficial, not only for the clergy spouses but for all members of a parsonage family, and for the church as a whole.

Carol and I both feel we would not make it as clergy wives if we didn't have a true friend in each other. We can tell each other everything and know the other will keep it in her heart. We need someone to chit-chat with and tell little things to and talk out any frustrations we might have (and sometimes there are many). When we get together we have the deepest joy of a friendship anyone could ever have. We love the same things, believe in the same values, love to shop, sing, talk, and eat.

Carol & Pat

We love life and love it even more when we are together with our family. Over the years our family has evolved into a great circle of friendship between the two families. All our children, grandchildren and great-grandchildren are under one umbrella. You couldn't ask for anything better than that.

Chapter 12

MOVE THAT UMBRELLA OVER, PLEASE

Pat

"I hope this is Gary's last move," I sighed. I was feeling sad about leaving our home in St. Louis, even though Gary and I like living in Florida and Gary was settling well into the new church.

It felt good that my best friend Carol could be here with me from Michigan to help me pack and sell some things in a big moving sale. She had shared so much of my life; it was only fitting. My eyes welled up, and tears rolled down my face. I had been having spells of tears all week. They came when I thought of the people in my life all along the way.

Carol came in from the deck and said, "Hey, Pat, where are you? I'm hungry. What do you want to eat?"

"Why don't we make some sandwiches?"

At the kitchen table I confessed to Carol. "I haven't gotten as much packing done as I thought I would. I got to looking at pictures and thinking about the old days."

Between bites, Carol chatted about what she and David had been talking about on the phone so long that morning.

"He was updating me on people in the church, the kids, grandkids and his garden. Did you know he loves to work in his garden now?"

"Somehow, it's hard to picture the David I knew working in the garden," I chuckled.

"I know. It seems strange. David loves his garden, his pond, fountain and his bog. You can't believe the enjoyment we both get out of watching the birds in the winter and summer. Are we getting old or what?"

We looked at each other and laughed.

"Oh, Pat, I'm going to miss our good times. You're always joking, and we have such a good time together."

We started cleaning up the kitchen.

As we worked, Carol asked me, "Have you and Gary really moved thirteen times?"

"Oh, at least that many," I said. "Haven't you and David moved a few times?"

"Oh, you know we've been in Northern Michigan since 1987. We moved around East Lansing a little and then up north sixteen years ago, but it doesn't seem like we have moved at all."

I looked at my first husband's wife and said, "I can't believe that you and David have been up north that long already."

Carol glanced over at me quickly. I must have had a funny look on my face.

I was remembering that when David and I were married we had moved a lot. "I don't know why we had to be the ones to move so much," I said quietly.

"Where were all the places you and Gary have lived?" Carol asked. I think she was trying to distract me from any more sad thoughts.

"Well, let's see," I said. "After we dated a couple of months, we got married and he moved into my condo out in DeWitt. Don't forget we had known each other for a while before we started our relationship," I laughed. "From there, we bought a house on Willow Street that we totally gutted and remodeled."

"Oh, yeah," Carol said. "I remember that place. It could have been a before-and-after house in Better Homes and Gardens."

"We put so much work into that house! What a great place it turned out to be," I said. "In fact, I think we had a couple of bridal showers there for our soon-to-be daughters-in law, remember?"

"I remember well," Carol said, smiling.

"Then we moved to New York when Gary felt a call from God to start attending General Theological Seminary. This was one of the hardest times for me, leaving my boys and my first grandchild. I remember they came to say good-bye. Little Joshua was only four weeks old and Elijah was soon to be born. I cried all the way to the Big Apple. But I really got to love it there and to this day I miss it. Our life at seminary was wonderful."

"That was a shock to all of us." Carol laughed. "When we found out that Gary was going to be an Episcopal priest, and you were going to be the wife of a priest—we were all so surprised! I remember loving all those trips we made with the kids to New York to see you and Gary. That last trip was pretty special when Gary graduated and was ordained and asked David to come and be one of his sponsors."

Gary's graduation and ordination was indeed a milestone in the family. It was made even better when Mark, David, Carol, and Greg were all there.

"You know we didn't know then that we both were going to be married to ministers!" Carol laughed. "I know that after we became Christians our relationship was so much closer." Changing the subject she said, "Tell me about your first pastorate again."

"Don't you remember?" I said. "We were in a wonderful parish for five years in Owosso, Michigan. Remember our great get-togethers for Christmas and birthdays with you and David and the kids? One of the things about our friendship that the kids always talked about was how cool it was to have everyone together and not feel any friction. Do you remember how many times David's brothers and sisters and their wives or husbands came with you and we would have a night out? Remember the Showboat in Chesaning? Both Gary and I loved the great times bringing the youth groups up to your place for ski trips. As I recall, your son John had a thing for one of the girls from our youth group and she for him."

"John was a good-looking guy and, hey, he still is," Carol laughed.

"Don't forget you're talking about my stepson!" I said.

Carol said, "I think he really enjoyed it when we had groups up for ski trips or canoe trips. Our place up north was so perfect for retreats, wasn't it? Didn't you go to Texas next?"

Our time in Owosso was over. Gary had accepted a call to a much larger church in Odessa, Texas. "That was a huge parish," I told Carol. "It had two churches, a school and a nursing home. Those were some very good times but also some hard times. You can please some people some of the time but you cannot please all the people all of the time!" I said shaking my head.

We poured steaming mugs of coffee and went back into the living room where the boxes were waiting for us.

I was still in a down-the-memory-lane kind of mood and wanted to reminisce. "One of my favorite memories is when you and David's sister Char and her friend Sharon came out and visited us. Charlene was battling cancer at the time and didn't have much energy. But we ended up having a great time shopping, eating, laughing, running into Clint Black and getting posters signed like schoolgirls. Then there was our trip down to Big Bend National Park and the Rio Grande. Char would have really enjoyed that if she were feeling better."

"I'll never forget that trip," Carol said. "Before we met up with you, the three of us spent two days in San Antonio. We

MOVE THAT UMBRELLA OVER, PLEASE

Charlene, Carol, Pat and Sharon in Texas

shopped, ate and went to the movies. San Antonio is a wonderful town."

"Yeah," I said, "I wish you would have invited me on that trip too!" As we hugged our coffee mugs I got serious as I thought about our days in Texas.

"I think my health was the worst in Texas," I told Carol. "And, of course, there was that incident with my sister. I will always appreciate Gary for making the decision to leave Texas so my health wouldn't get worse with all the stress we were under. That move cost us a lot. We ended up in East Lansing, Michigan, and Gary didn't have a parish job for at least a year. That's when he decided to get into interim work. Who would have thought that we would be moving every two or three years after that?

"That's when you and I became so close. I've always felt fortunate to have you as a friend. Not only were you a good friend, but you became a mother to my boys and a wonderful grandma to our grandkids. Better than I was at the time, because we were always moving so we didn't see the kids as much as we would have liked. Oh, the kids always came to visit wherever we were, but we missed so many birthdays, special days at school, so many holidays and everything else parents and grandparents do. But somehow we've stayed close knit, haven't we?"

Carol looked at me and smiled warmly. I had told her before what her friendship meant to me and how important her role as a step-mom has been, but it doesn't hurt to say it again.

"You know I always knew I wasn't the mother of your boys," Carol said. "But I absolutely felt that I was a grandma to their kids. You know before I came here I dug out some old pictures. We have so many pictures of David and me and the grandkids when they were young. We sure did a lot of fun things with them. Now that they are grown it gives us real joy that John has three little girls and we again try to do fun things. It's a little harder since they live in Florida. I love it too that you and Gary can go and visit John and his family even when we're not down there."

"Oh," I said, "we love seeing the girls too! With us being so close and them in Fort Meyers and us in Fort Lauderdale, we can share a lot of special days together. Those girls—what a handful!" I laughed. Do you remember how you and I would babysit for a week or more while John and Chris would do a get-away? It took the two of us to get the job done."

"When you were in East Lansing," Carol said, "David finished his schooling and was ordained as the pastor of Bear Lake Christian Church. I call it our little log church in the wildwood," she said fondly. "It was the coldest day of the year—below zero—and David had to go pick up some of our people because their cars wouldn't start. Somehow we had a large crowd there to witness him being officially ordained by six ministers—including your Gary. It was wonderful that the guys asked each other to take part in their ordinations, wasn't it?"

I nodded, thinking about the times our paths had intersected.

"How did it go when you and Gary started your interim pastorates?" Carol asked me.

"Our first job was at Bay City, Michigan. We loved that rectory—it was big, old and stylish. It even had a fourth floor ballroom. The people were so nice and that was a good change from where we came from in Texas! That's when you and I got into the clothing business, remember?"

"Oh, do I remember," Carol said as we drained our coffee mugs. "Boy, didn't we have fun! The work was hard, but I've never laughed as hard. Do you remember the times we'd practically wet our pants laughing? Remember how we'd set up our craft tent and have a great time selling our stock? I loved visiting great cities in Michigan and staying overnight for the two-day shows and eating our hearts out. You'd thought we would have lost weight! We carried all those grids, put up the tent, and had that stock out in record time. By doing that almost every weekend we should have both been skinny!"

I said, "Don't forget how when we were out overnight, we couldn't wait to get back to our room to relax, count the money, and eat our carry-out food after 'sizing up' at the nearest drive-through."

I was on a roll. "From there we went to Port Huron, Michigan. I think that was one of Gary's favorite places. He did a lot of sailing there with one of our parishioners. Of course, I wasn't there much because you and I were on the road doing craft shows with our clothing line. 'Those were the days my friend'; too bad they had to end! Well, they ended, didn't they? I know our husbands were glad that Gary's next church took us to St. Louis, Missouri. Remember how sad we were when we had to sell our craft tent, all our grids and our stock? We sold everything down to every last tee shirt and sweat shirt.

"I was sad when you guys moved," Carol said. "But at least you came back to Michigan a lot. That first St. Louis parish was a great church for you. Wasn't it a very well-to-do congregation?"

"Yes, it was."

"David and I, and my mom and dad really enjoyed driving out to see you the end of April in 1999 and taking that side trip to Branson. My mom always mentioned how for those five days she had no pain from her cancer. I was glad she got to make the trip before she died that August. I was glad when my dad wanted to make the trip again in October of 1999 to visit. That was another fun time. You had a lot of the family visit you there, didn't you?"

"Oh yes, and we loved it anytime someone came." Once again I had tears in my eyes. "It gets lonely moving so much and you can't help but miss your kids, grandkids and parents when they live so far from you. It was nice when family visited because it was special time together, time with just them. Not that it isn't fun when we all get together! But you know how it is, we all talk at the same time and no one listens.

"I was excited when after St. Louis we got another church in Michigan. I couldn't wait to get back. I loved that church in Birmingham, Michigan. It was only hours away from our mom's place and sister's, the kids, and, of course, you and David. I know Gary loved it.

"But he was probably doubtful when I announced that I wanted to start doing craft shows with our handmade jewelry with you and Ginger. Isn't she the greatest daughter-in-law?" I asked Carol. "I can still hear Gary warning me not to get us into debt like the last time you and I were in business together."

"Isn't that a husband for you? Carol laughed. "David said the same thing. I know those two never understood why we got into debt the first time around."

"Well, I do!" I said, remembering that I got a job selling women's clothing when we moved back to Michigan from Texas and then to Bay City. I carried three lines of clothing and traveled on the road to different stores. "It was fun and I met a lot of nice people. I loved it when I had to travel up north and I could stay at your place. I even got you to go with me on some calls, remember?"

"Sure," Carol said. "I went to that cute shop in Elk Rapids. The hardest thing was wheeling those clothing racks into that small shop."

"I especially missed being in business with you." Carol and I enjoyed working together so much that we decided to manufacture some of our own clothing and take it on the road with my other lines.

Carol laughed, "Do you remember making 500 embellished Santa sweatshirts? We had sweatshirts all over the place and paint all over us. We'd work into the wee hours, eat, laugh and paint until we dropped!"

"Our husbands did think we were a bit off the wall, didn't they, Carol? Just think, we had 500 to do with a two-week turnaround time! Makes me shiver to think of it."

Pictures of our last 2 of 500

"I think we came to our senses then," Carol said, "thought about it and knew there was a better way to make money besides being the middleman."

I thought about our next decision to do craft shows, starting with winter ones that were inside and the next year outside with our new craft tent and other equipment. That's what got us into debt—buying equipment and building our inventory.

"Oh, remember when we went to get the craft tent? We drove to Detroit and met that guy Jerry we knew from the craft shows. Remember how after a short course in tents we took our four walls, one top and a million clips and pipes and bungies and headed for home? We were so excited when we got there. We went over to the side yard between your place and mom and dad's place and started to practice putting up the tent. Hours and hours and up and down with the walls and the next day we started again and after six hours we finally got it to work. Your mom would come over and bring us water and yes, a little food, but we never quit until we got it right, no matter how much we rolled on the ground laughing. Then there was our inventory. We had one or two pieces of each size and color to please all our customers, but that cost money. We did make a lot more money but it was hard getting that debt down."

"Well, no wonder," Carol said. "We were definitely taking our share for working and paying our expenses. I think if we could have stayed in business a couple more years, our husbands wouldn't have needed to bail us out at the end."

"I think so too," I said. "Remember when the four of us got together and came up with our company name? I will never forget it—Raspberry Creek, Ltd. I am so glad you thought to take the picture of us with our company shirts on when the four of us went on a trip together to the Upper Peninsula. We laughed so hard as we walked into that restaurant together, thinking everyone was laughing at us for having the same shirts on. Of course, we were the only ones laughing."

We had tears in our eyes from laughing so hard. It was just as funny the second time around. Carol said, "If it's true that the more you laugh, the longer you live, then you and I will definitely both have a long life."

David/Carol and Pat/Gary Raspberry Creek Shirts

"Okay, now where were we?" I said, trying to pull myself together. "We were in Birmingham and just about ready to start craft shows with our daughter-in-law, Ginger. It's funny how all three of us started making jewelry but neither one of us knew the other one was doing it too." Birmingham had brought us within distance again of family and our friendship. We just picked up where we left off. We designed and made our own jewelry and then shared a booth and tables at a few craft shows.

"I think David and Gary became even closer after that," Carol said. "I loved our trips together, the four of us. There were the island trips: Drummond Island, Beaver Island, St. Joseph's Island, and Sugar Island. Remember the time David and I came to stay with you guys at your Birmingham apartment? We did the Detroit tour, hockey town, the people mover, down the river on the Canadian side spotting those freighters."

"You and your love of freighters," I said. "I have never known anyone to get so excited when they see a freighter go by."

"I know," Carol agreed. "I can't help it. The memories go back into my childhood when my grandpa, who was a professional photographer, would take my brother and me to Port Huron or Marine City to spend the day at the park, while he took pictures of the freighters passing by. I just love those freighters! It was so great having you back in Michigan, and fun every time you'd come up north to do a craft show. Gary was really understanding about that, wasn't he?"

"Yes, he has been great through all of our ventures together."

"David, too," Carol said. "I know it was a little harder on you because David definitely did not like me missing a Sunday at church to do a craft show. I tried booking mostly Saturday shows, and when they were on weekends you always handled it until I could get there. At least when we were doing our jewelry, Ginger was there with you."

Carol gave a glance around at the work that wasn't getting done and asked, "You must be getting to the end of the story of all your moves aren't you?"

"Not quite," I laughed. "Our next move brought us back to St. Louis where we bought this house. We love this place and even though it was brand new, we put a lot of extras into it. Our neighbors are great, always ready to do anything for us."

"I remember meeting your neighbors when David and I and Mark, Ginger and Charity came that year for Thanksgiving along with Mitch, Josh and Jennifer from Florida. Wasn't it great to have most of the family together? Those were some of the pictures I found. Charity was in one, coloring her Uncle Mitch's hair. We had a good time," Carol said, smiling.

"Little did we know that when we bought this house we would be moving so soon," I said. After our interim position was over, Gary was called to a position in Palm Harbor, Florida, close to Mitch and his family. I was excited about that. After all those years, we could finally live close to one of our kids.

"That was a hard move as we had the house. We decided to keep it, not knowing where we would go after Palm Harbor. Gary moved down there and I moved up north into one of your chalets to work with our oldest son, Mark, and David and do craft shows with you and Ginger. That was a busy summer, wasn't it?"

"It sure was," Carol agreed. "That was when we started our deck-building business."

"Well, I don't know if I would call it a business, but we did build two decks for Mark."

"I still can't believe you and I did that, Pat. I had never even held a drill before or carried lumber or anything. It was just about the greatest feeling, accomplishing something that was so much out of character for me. Now, ask me to balance your checkbook, type minutes, do bookkeeping, or something like that and I say 'no problem.' You were the one with the know-how and experience, Pat. We laughed hard quite a few times getting those projects done."

"Didn't we always laugh and have a good time whatever we did?" I said. "Even in a bad situation, we always made the best of it.

"So, Palm Harbor it was, and I think I finally got down there in the fall after Gary had been there all summer. We seemed to fall into the lifestyle pretty easily. We spent a lot of time with our youngest son Mitch and his wife Janis as well as our four grandkids, Mitch's two, Josh and Jennifer and Janis' two, Lauren and Anthony. Especially me, since I started working with Mitch in his home improvement business where Jennifer worked as well. I enjoyed those days. It didn't hurt our friendship either, since

Josh, Carol, Pat
Family at Mitch's House in Florida, Gary, Matt, David, Mark, Mitch, John

you guys have a place just two hours south of Mitch. Since John was down there too, you were in Florida on a regular basis.

"Our latest move was to Fort Lauderdale just this year. That's when we decided to sell this house. We were thankful when it finally did sell since it's been sitting here for the last couple years with no one here. And here we are now, with the movers on the way. Have I told you how much I appreciate you coming from Michigan to help me and keep me company?" I knew it was hard for Carol to be with me right then as her father wasn't well.

"I was glad to come and help," Carol said. "You know he felt better the day I left to come. He actually insisted I come. What are friends for? You certainly have done a lot for me over the years. Ours is definitely an unusual friendship. It's no wonder that so many of our customers who bought our clothing and got to know us told us to write a book. I've been thinking about it...the book needs to tell people that forgiveness is possible in divorce, and friendship is even better."

I couldn't agree more.

On days when the world threatens rain and storms, our umbrella protects, and guides us into forgiveness and friendship.

AFTERWORD: SOMEWHERE OVER THE RAINBOW

PAT AND CAROL

Why did we feel that we needed to share the story of our lives as friends? Partly it was because we were urged to do so by many friends who found our story inspiring. It was also because we wanted to pass down a legacy to our family. We want them to know how we came to feel this way. And yes, it is with the hope that someday they or their children and on down the line can see what a difference love and forgiveness has made in their lives.

We look back on our lives as parents and hope our children have good memories and thoughts about a home that was not perfect, but loving. The homes we remember have long been made into somebody else's homes. But we hope that our children, Mark, Matthew, Mitch, John, Greg and Vickie will look back in time and think of the fun and loving times they had as they grew up. The same goes for our grandchildren, great-grandchildren, and on and on. They are all dear to us because a little of our blood is in their veins. The melody of our lives will go on singing through our children.

We hope this story will let our children and grandchildren know they were loved. The four of us want them to know that the friendship we shared was in part to help them understand that forgiveness makes a difference.

We believe in our life as friends. God had a plan for us. How else could a friendship like ours touch so many? How is it possible that people can divorce and break up families and come back together? How is it possible that parents and children from different families can still become one family? Our family is the most precious thing of all, and we've all lived under one umbrella!

It's love that has done it. Love for each other. Think of it…fifty-one years later that umbrella is still up. The love is still there. Yes, we've weathered some bad storms, but there's never been a hole or tear in our relationship (umbrella). Our extended family has grown. Many more children later, the umbrella has never been too small to shield us all.

There are days when our faith in God is strong and sustaining. There are other days when we cry out to God for His umbrella to cover us and keep us safe and get us through our pain. One thing is for sure. If you look back at our lives and see how things turned out then you must know there is a God.

All four of us wish for all of you that along the way you may meet someone who will be to you the delight you all have been to us. Thanks for reading our story. Send it to a friend. It may help someone see that forgiveness and love is possible in a blended family. God has blessed us all.

As ever,
Pat and Carol and, yes, Gary and David

Pleasant Word

To order additional copies of this title call:
1-877-421-READ (7323)
or please visit our web site at
www.pleasantwordbooks.com

If you enjoyed this quality custom published book,
drop by our web site for more books and information.

www.winepressgroup.com
"Your partner in custom publishing."

Printed in the United States
88600LV00001B/163-189/A